I0480236

Rigged Money

The Fateful Lure of Fiat Money

2nd Edition

Detlef Gloge PhD

BookLocker
Trenton, Georgia

Published by BookLocker.com, Inc., Trenton, Georgia.

BookLocker.com, Inc.
2024

Second Edition

Library of Congress Cataloguing in Publication Data
Gloge PhD, Detlef
Rigged Money, 2nd Edition: The Fateful Lure of Fiat Money
by Detlef Gloge PhD
Library of Congress Control Number: 2024909166

Disclaimer

This book details the author's opinions about economic subjects. The author is not a licensed financial consultant. The author and the publisher make no representations or warranties of any kind with respect to this book or its content. The author and the publisher disclaim all such warranties of financial advice for a particular purpose and don't warrant that the information accessible via this book is accurate, complete, or current.

Please consult with your own certified public accountant or financial services professional regarding the suggestions and recommendations made in this book. Neither the author nor the publisher will be liable for damages arising out of or in connection with use of this book. This is a comprehensive limitation of liability that applies to all damages, including (without limitation) compensatory, direct, indirect, or consequential damages; loss of data, income, or profit; loss of or damage to property; and third-party claims.

You should understand that this book isn't intended as a substitute for consultation with a licensed financial professional. This book provides content related to topics on finance and economic living. As such, use of this book implies your acceptance of this disclaimer.

Table of Contents

About the Book

Money injected into the economic process behaves in rather logical ways. Bankers know this but won't tell you. Read the stories in this book. Over time, for example, money adjusts to the things we trade. If the Federal Reserve (the Fed) prints more money than we trade, inflation destroys existing purchasing power, your wealth and mine.

Often, the Fed prints excess money to assist the government, which likes to borrow but hates to pay interest. The Fed then charges the government an interest rate equal to the inflation rate. The result is that your wealth and mine pays the government's interest. It is a kind of excess tax you and I don't know about, $1.3 trillion during the last two decades.

What is more, the government's debt loses purchasing power equal to the inflation rate. That means if the government ever pays its debt, it will repay $1.3 trillion less than it borrowed. Don't think the government is the Fed's only preferred client. This book also explains how the elites grow rich while middle class living standards decline. Or find out how the Fed counterfeits mouse-click money on its computers.

About the Author

Rigged Money is provocative, incisive, and honest. The author is concerned about wealth inequality, debt, stagnation, and the growing crescendo of public frustration with U.S. monetary policy. Observing the increasing deluge of money, he is appalled by government expansion and how inflation despoils the most vulnerable in society. He traces these conditions back to the 1913 banking reform, which upended the Founding Fathers' constitutional mandates.

The author has maintained an uncompromising independence from the dissonance and confusion in the economic field. His common sense and independent mind stem from his training as a PhD in engineering and mathematics. Six dozen publications and patents bear his name. The Bell Laboratories team that he led deployed the first prototype Internet links. He is a fellow of the U.S. Engineering Society and a member of the National Academy of Sciences.

The book's objectivity is a refreshing contrast to mainstream duplicity on this subject. His lucid arguments contrast with the usual academic jargon and sophistry, so they should appeal to anyone with common sense and social awareness. The author explains the founders' constitutional concept of sound money, how citizens have twice impelled the U.S. Congress to adhere to it, and why the time has come for another regress.

The author's accomplishments have shaped his desire to join those who openly express their concerns for our future and recommend changes. The themes he highlights in this book are a progression from his earlier books, *How Not to Make Money, Money Forensics,* and an earlier Edition of *Rigged Money.* This book is his most unreserved, candid exposition of the surreptitious harm and inequity inflicted on society by fractional reserve banking and fiat money.

Rigged Money is for those who care about the future of the United States. It's also a wake-up call for politicians who keep looking the other way while monetary malpractice is tearing the country apart. The author concludes the book with recommendations for the changes that the U.S. must make to remain a leader in a changing multipolar world.

Preface:
The Coup of the Century

The American colonists resented British banking practices, and some left England for this very reason. Thomas Jefferson wrote to a friend: *And I sincerely believe with you, that banking establishments are more dangerous than standing armies and that the principle of spending money to be paid by posterity under the name of funding is but swindling futurity on a large scale.* [1]

In Britain, currency debasement and inflation had caused egregious wealth inequality. The Bank of England rigged the currency by counterfeiting paper notes. English administrators even tried to affect the Revolutionary War by counterfeiting the colonists' *dollars.*

The Founding Fathers considered counterfeiting a crime as heinous as treason. They wanted sound money to be freely available to all and wrote in the Constitution: *No state shall make any Thing but gold and silver coins.* Yet today, U.S. wealth inequality and contempt for the underclass are no different than they were in Britain.

When Congress chartered the First Bank of the United States, Jefferson wrote: *The Bank of the United States is one of the most-deadly hostilities existing against the principles and form of our Constitution.* [2] The bank existed only from 1791 to 1811. Congress chartered the Second Bank of the

United States in 1816 but abrogated it in 1836 after its note issuance caused the Western land rush.

The Civil War finally compelled the U.S. to pass the Bank Act of 1863, which abandoned sound money, introduced reserve banking, and the printing of paper notes, which created the exorbitant quantities of money needed for the war. Congress also introduced the income tax and a harbinger of the Secret Service, which tracked down nongovernment counterfeiters. As had happened in Europe, wars relinquished sound money and sound banking.

Nearly 50 years later, the 16th Amendment codified the income tax, and the Federal Reserve Act legalized peacetime reserve banking. In so doing, the 1913 coup, which legislated today's U.S. money and banking, overstepped constitutional restrictions on federal authority—the General Welfare Clause and the Commerce Clause—which specifically limited these authorities to the states.

The result was a banking cartel and a central bank which bankers named the *Federal Reserve*, implying that it served the public, rather than the bankers who profit from it. In short, they established a system that the founders had vowed to avoid.

It turned out to be an easy con: Bureaucrats and politicians were caught off guard; Congress ignored its constitutional responsibilities; and the 1913 Federal Reserve Act left Americans in the dark about bankers' intentions. As John K. Galbraith remarked: *The study of money, above all other fields of economics, is the one in which complexity is used to disguise the truth or evade the truth, not to reveal it.* [3]

Since then, economists have been flocking to the Federal Reserve's Eccles Building in Washington. Ryan Grim writes: *The Federal Reserve, through its extensive network of consultants, visiting scholars, alumni, and staff economists so thoroughly dominates the field of economics that real criticism of the central bank has become a career liability for members of the profession.* [4]

The *Roaring Twenties* provided the first sign of the money deluge to come when American loans for World War I opened the floodgates for money creation. Offshore banks later added trillions of Eurodollars. By the '70s, the dollar was a fiat currency backed by nothing but faith and trust in the Fed and the government. All currencies floated freely. The world's central banks started the *race to the bottom* by debasing their currencies and flooding the world with credit.

Today, sound money based on a stable money supply no longer exists. Banking cartels worldwide create abundant fiat money, which enriches bankers, impoverishes cash users, and thereby destroys the social fabric. Past periods of the gold standard are evidence that only the enforcement of sound money guarantees healthy economies and societies.

Many Americans consider money creation a legitimate right of the banking profession. Technically,

however, money creation is a form of counterfeiting, which infringes on citizens' property rights.

Part One explains how money should and shouldn't be used, starting with counterfeiting. Chapter 1 introduces sound money as the legitimate basis for all commerce through the example of Say's law. Chapter 2 asks why free markets need a Federal Reserve that dictates interest rates. Chapter 3 examines the creation of money through fractional reserve banking. Chapters 4 and 5 explain how banks abuse money and profit from it.

Part One:
The Money Game

Valid banknotes have an intrinsic value equal to the goods and services for which the banknotes can be exchanged. Thus, the intrinsic value of a nation's money supply varies with its tradable wealth. Production and thrift increase intrinsic value, while consumption and waste dilute and debase it.

The U.S. government's Bureau of Engraving and Printing prints banknotes, and the Federal Reserve authorizes the printing and issuing of these notes, which are marked *Federal Reserve Notes*. The Fed also creates money by computer keystroke which is equally valid and interchangeable with Federal Reserve Notes.

Neither action adds wealth or intrinsic value to the money supply. The outcome is therefore that the money creation dilutes and debases the existing money supply and that money holders suffer price inflation and purchasing power loss—albeit with a delay of a year or two.

Thus, the Fed counterfeits money into existence. Today's money game is played with fiat money, which imposes no constraints on the Fed's counterfeiting, so it depends entirely on the Fed's activity whether the Fed sustains or destroys trust in today's fiat dollars.

To prepare the reader for what Galbraith calls *disguising or evading truth about money*, the next two chapters illustrate some of the complexities of money creation. Chapter 1 examines inflation, money debasement, wealth inequality, business cycles, recessions, debts, and depressions.

Chapter 2 focuses on the Federal Reserve, which originally was meant to serve as banks' lender of last resort, and now uses its power to counterfeit money and dictate the nationwide cost of credit. Guided by the *Federal Open Market Committee* and goaded by government fiscal policy, the Fed is the guardian of the trust in the fiat dollar.

With this background, Chapter 3 explains *fractional reserve banking*, a process that the Federal Reserve and its member banks use to expand the money supply and lend money to active borrowers who circulate it in the economy.

The remaining chapters of Part One demonstrate why and how the banking cartel forged in 1913 has gone so spectacularly astray. Part Two argues how sound money could save nations from the present calamity. Part Three focuses on how money affects global relations. Part Four examines present banking and government practices, why fiat money is provoking a dangerous path, and what the U.S. must do to preserve its financial health.

Chapter 1:
Market Laws

To understand how money circulates in markets, imagine a barter market: A group of traders offers people promissory notes that people can use to browse among the group's products. The traders specify the notes' value. The choices and flexibility that this idea offers give the group an advantage over their competitors' barter trades.

Similarly, today's markets use money notes, which circulate and are reused after a given turnover period. Producers try to sell what they have produced during the turnover period. They set prices so that people's incomes earned during the turnover period cover the sales. The process works because consumers and workers are the same people, participating in production or supplying resources to it. Therefore, their earnings (producers' costs) provide income to purchase production.

The Frenchman Jean Baptiste Say was the first to describe this process. It's now called *Say's law,* a maxim of classical economics. [5] The law governs all commerce based on so-called *sound money*, whose aggregate quantity and unit value is immutable.

When banks add money, they change the quantity and dilute and debase all existing units. They add money out of concern that money scarcity might slow commerce. Keynes, for example, called for banks and governments to inject money whenever economic demand weakens. Yet there are other views. Murray Rothbard wrote, *there is never a social need for banks to increase the supply of money.*[6]

The fact is that the money supply can shrink and expand over a certain range without upsetting the economy because people always hold a cushion of liquidity as a buffer. On the other hand, banks' excessive and rapid money expansion causes credit booms and asset bubbles, and intense money shrinkage leads to insolvencies and domino chains of bankruptcies which end in debt and deflation.

For example, during the post-Civil-War era from 1865 to1879, authorities shrank the wartime money supply. Wealth grew, prices fell, and purchasing power increased, earning everyone a salient growth dividend. Chapters 6 describes the era in detail: U.S. growth was the highest in the Republic's history.

Milton Friedman and Anna Schwartz wrote: *From 1865 to 1879, the price level fell to half its initial level, and [US] economic growth proceeded at a rapid rate. This coincidence casts serious doubts at the validity of the now widely held view that secular price deflation and rapid economic growth are incompatible.* [7]

The *widely held view* to which the authors refer is the banks' claim that deflation increases the risk of loan defaults and that banks must create money until deflation turns into 2% inflation. This action shifts the growth dividend from the public to banks and increases bank lending, bank profits, inflation, and U.S. wealth inequality.

Richard Cantillon describes inflation as follows: *The first to use new money are not affected by inflation but incite it to harm everybody else.*[8] His point is that early bank borrowers invest in capital assets at uninflated prices, but the accruing inflation later debases unsuspecting consumers' cash.

The government has a bureau that monitors basic consumer prices. Accurate inflation indices are based not only on these prices, but also on asset prices, taxes, credit, mortgage debt, insurance, and other costs, to name just a few. The bureau's policy since 1983 has been to select and adjust input data that understate the published inflation index. [9]

Banks use the bureau's inflation index as their inflation target. Because the bureau understates the index, banks create more than 2% inflation to match the understated index value at 2%. Hence, accumulating inflation grows for years at more than 2% while the public is fed the 2% myth.

To beat inflation, the rich buy assets, which retain their value. Hence, asset prices rise as the currency loses value. Some invest in productive businesses and amass fortunes. But those who earn and spend their cash just see their own incomes shrink.

> The top 1% own 34% of U.S. wealth.
> The bottom 50% own barely 2.6%.

America's growth dividend could have enriched the entire population, but bank money caused contentious wealth inequality which slowly crushed people's faith in prosperity and the American dream.

Murray Rothbard and the American founders believed in the advantages of sound money, which had served America well during the first century of the Republic. By 1913, U.S. industrialization needed a centralized money-clearing system. It seemed therefore reasonable to adopt the fractional reserve system of the Europeans, which networked all banks in a cartel, as Chapter 3 describes in detail.

This meant adjusting to money debasement and inflation. These distortions affect the entire economy—not just consumer goods and services, but all assets, real and financial. Debasement meant that a dollar earned 50 years ago is today worth a few cents. Saving for old age has become a fool's errand.

Governments have many ways of using inflation to exploit their citizens. Nations build industrial capacity, underprice exports, or undermine competitors' industries by debasing their citizens' money. **Chinese Premier Deng Xiaoping was so impressed by the Western banking approach that he made it the centerpiece of Chinese state capitalism in the 1980s.**

Banks have a long history of taking advantage of people's money. When people tried to protect themselves by using precious metal coins, banks offered to hold the coins in custody and issued more paper notes than they had coins in custody. This abuse led to the *gold standard*, which limited money creation to a nation's gold ownership, a limit which confined money creation to sound money.

World War I ended the gold standard. The U.S. devalued the dollar, confiscated its citizens' gold, and declared the gold-backed dollar the global reserve currency. [10]

When the U.S. defaulted on its gold redemptions in 1971, it turned the dollar and all other affiliated currencies into **fiat** *money* whose value depends entirely on the issuing nations' **inclination to fiat (create)** money. The U.S. maximizes its latitude to create dollars by rewarding nation, such as the OPEC members, to use it for trading. Their use created the nickname *petrodollar.*

The global dollar trade was a boon for U.S. banks, because it accelerated money growth and bank profits. But as Americans borrowed to buy foreign goods, the growing imports slowly crippled U.S. production and employment.

Thus, U.S. conditions deteriorated. Prior to 1913, Americans had owned their money, saved, invested, and increased productivity. Nobody inflated away people's wealth or bootstrapped prices to capricious levels. People lent their savings to those who produced more wealth. Today, repressive money rates, fierce bank competition, relentless taxation, and Keynesian prejudice against thrift have all but eradicated savings in America.

Corrupting money by dilution and expansion has various negative side effects. The next chapter adds to this list by explaining how after 1913, banks surreptitiously usurped the money supply, skimmed funds from the productive sector, lured people into personal debt and financial dependence, and even coerced them to pay for the government's debt.

Chapter 2:
Manipulator in Chief

Wary of European banking practices, America's founders specified in the Constitution that *Congress shall have the Power to coin money and regulate the value thereof ... and that no state ... shall make any Thing but gold and silver Coin as Tender in Payment of Debt.* The founders wanted money to be sound, freely available to all, and unencumbered by manipulation. Their currency of choice was initially the Spanish silver dollar, then later the *greenback*, a paper dollar that was redeemable in gold. The public owned the money and could buy more by paying the issuer the intrinsic value.

A century later, in 1913, New York bankers wrangled control of the currency from the government, lobbying Congress to pass the Federal Reserve Act, which aimed to replicate the European way of banking, i.e., its cartel structure and the massive profits bankers earned from creating and lending money. [11]

To this end, they wanted a central bank that had the legal authority to manipulate the national lending rate, create and abrogate credit, and buy (monetize) government debt. They called it the *Federal Reserve* (*Fed*, for short), pretending that it served the public, rather than the cartel's bankers.

The timing was perfect: Europe needed loans to fight in World War I—an opportunity for the Fed to expand the money supply and for banks to profit.[12] The Fed's lending binge continued through the Roaring Twenties creating credit for speculators that inflated a huge asset bubble. When it burst in 1929, nonperforming loans bankrupted debtors and banks.

Alan Greenspan wrote later that *the excess credit which the Fed pumped into the [U.S.] economy spilled over into the stock market triggering a fantastic speculative boom.*[13] Adolph Miller, a member of the Federal Reserve's board, told the Senate Committee on Banking and Currency: *It has never yet been demonstrated that any agency can be invented to which the power to govern the currency could be entrusted without ultimately disastrous consequences.* [14]

Yet the Fed had ulterior motives for the massive expansion and debasement of the currency: It quickly devalued the greenbacks that Americans had owned before 1913. After that, the only money of value left was credit offered by banks. Without people noticing it, banks changed ownership of American money.

Banks claimed that, based on Roman contract law, they own all deposits and have the right to charge interest when they lend them. Soon, all money was cartel money, and the Fed decided to expand or contract the quantity by adjusting the funds rate.

The European banking conventions date back centuries, when European bankers, jewelers, and pawnbrokers invented today's money creation, which gave rise to the famous motto: ***Let me issue and control a nation's money, and I care not who writes the laws.***[15]

Today, inflation targeting has increased the bank-created money supply massively. Lending continuously increases the supply, while inflation dilutes its value, enriching borrowers, and impoverishing consumers. By depressing the funds rate, the Fed encourages consumers, the government, and other unproductive borrowers to boost banking activity and profits.

Excessive lending causes rollercoaster boom-and-bust cycles, which grow and shrink credit, kindled by the Fed's rate manipulations. The U.S. experienced no less than a dozen such business cycles since the end of WWII. Banks skim massive windfall profits from the productive sector and fund their own ventures, competing with rich clients and other banks.

> Banks' massive profit retention drains the productive sector of resources.

Jeremy Grantham, founder of GMO Asset Management, speaks of the debilitating drain to which these cycles subject private enterprise: *The U.S. financial sector is, in a way, like a giant bloodsucker…. What we have done is created layers upon layers of more convoluted expensive financial instruments…. And it's taken a lot of ingenuity and salesmanship to make this happen, a lot of lobbying in Congress, etc. And we have imposed on the rest of the economy the idea that banking and finance are utterly important: If you do anything wrong to us, the entire economy will collapse in ragged disarray.* [16]

To demonstrate and preserve its independence, the Fed eagerly pleases the government by creating easy money and repressing the funds rate and savers' earnings. The Fed's cheap dollars employ millions of bureaucrats busy writing regulations that depress private sector productivity. The abundance of dollars also attracts imports, which bankrupt domestic producers and drive them abroad. Productivity declines as imports increase.

Years of low Fed funds rates have convinced people that low rates are here to stay and that they can borrow to replace maturing debt. Businesses borrow to buy back equity, *zombie* firms subsist on increasing debt, households rely on revolving credit, and students hope that their debt-financed education will make them rich.

The Fed's prolonged massive credit glut overleveraged banks and caused the 2008 Global Financial Crisis.[17] Fortunately, the Fed's massive bank bailout forestalled another depression, but the Fed's new counterfeiting gambit, so-called *quantitative easing at zero interest rates,* only postponed the economic meltdown.

The Fed continued its counterfeiting through the Covid pandemic, through massive inflation, a $50 trillion asset bubble, and a commercial real estate crisis. Excessive liquidity only dissipated after the Fed reversed its easy-money policy and deflated some of the public and private debt.

Still, U.S. national debt, public and private, stands at $94 trillion and grows daily by several billions. The federal government owes $34 trillion in Treasury debt and approximately $100 trillion in other liabilities, such as Social Security, Medicare, and Medicaid payments.

Undaunted by the $1 trillion gross interest that its creditors demand, the federal government, paralyzed by its own commitments, insists that the Fed monetize its debt with counterfeit dollars, hoping that trenchant inflation will shrink some of its liabilities.

To be sure, the dollar isn't the only overleveraged and indebted fiat currency: Since the crash of 1991 in Japan, that nation has grown its debt to ¥1.3 quadrillion, 263% of its GDP, encumbered by demographic decline. Unmanageable credit similarly leverages The Chinese nation. The common currency of the euro area obfuscates the credit relationships between its 20 members. Chapter 12 elaborates.

Measured in dollars, global debt now totals $315 trillion, close to three times global GDP. Counterfeiting and spending fiat money is a fateful lure that nobody can resist. The previous two chapters provide the reader with the background to understand what drives the world's banking cartels.

Chapter 3:
Money Out of Thin Air

Neither the U.S. Congress nor the rest of the federal government was prepared for the surprises of the fledgling banking cartel after its inauguration in 1913. As is now evident, bankers had decided all along to shift money ownership from citizens to banks, then manipulate rates and credit at their discretion.

To be sure, a more centralized banking network was going to benefit U.S. commerce. The cartel network allowed businesses and households to deposit dollars and settle their affairs at banks nationwide. If a borrower requested a loan, the bank simply credited the borrower's account with available deposit money. All commercial banks were part of the cartel structure and shared the risks of creating credit and lending it.

Technically, banks agreed to lend each other so-called *reserves*, with which they cover funds that borrowers or depositors expect in their accounts. Today, this process enables cartel banks to lend millions of dollars while the reserves involved total less than 10% of their deposits. This joint lending benefit is how the process came to be called *fractional reserve lending.*

Today, most banks keep their reserves at the Fed, which pays banks interest. Furthermore, banks protect themselves by owning capital and highly liquid assets. The interest to hold these funds determines banks' cost of money and borrowers' loan interest. The lower the rate, the more borrowers line up for bank credit. At recent low rates, U.S. bank credit and debt, public and private, total trillions of dollars.

The source of all this money is both the U.S. Treasury, which prints new banknotes, and the Fed, which counterfeits money by computer. The money created has no intrinsic value, but the Fed uses it to purchase Treasury notes, thereby rendering all seigniorage to the government.

This is the process colloquially called *creating money out of thin air*. It is fundamentally different from savings that are earned, not counterfeited, and cause no inflation. Banks are not involved in the productive process, so bank money is surplus money that corrupts Say's process and induces inflation, as Chapter 1 explained.

Investing and fostering productivity are the last things on banks' minds, as they focus on the bulk profits they earn from consumer borrowing. They grow the money supply 4–6% annually, whereas productivity today grows at 0–2% at most. The difference is inflation that devalues the dollar. Banks rescind all repaid loans but increase loan volume so that outstanding credit increases.

Accordingly, the dollar is now worth a fraction of its 1971 value. The richest 10% own 90% of all income-producing assets and have raised home prices and rents to levels few can afford. Inflation has decimated wages and incomes. The impoverished lower classes survive on government transfer payments. The economy is leveraged 5:1 with incomes inadequate to service the massive debt. This is exactly what the founders tried to avoid.

> Inflation devastates the middle class. Banks enrich Wall Street and the government.

Worse yet, excessive lending creates business cycles that upend the entire economy: Prices inflate, thereby debasing the money supply and shrinking purchasing power. The Fed raises rates, banks curtail lending, booms turn to busts, and recessions, layoffs, and distressing losses follow.

U.S. banks loan other people's income, get paid for risks they don't face, and charge monopoly prices to lend debased money. They siphon massive profits from the productive sector, which then stagnates, burdened by increasing debt. Offshore banks piggyback on U.S. domestic banks to lend Eurodollars to foreigners.

Chapter 4 describes the strategy that the money cartel has developed to inject and debase money loaned for profit, as well as steer inflation and growth.

Chapter 4:
Managing Growth

Prior to 1913, private savers provided the capital that supported America's industry and wealth. They lent their savings to producers, who needed capital to grow their businesses. The result was that the money supply grew with production and wealth.

Today, banks lend money to everyone—mostly consumers, speculators, and the government, which produce little or nothing. The result is that banks create money annually that loses purchasing power through inflation. To be sure, banks' massive lending may reach a few productive borrowers, but the rest of the populace continuously loses wealth, as inflation debases the cash in people's pockets.

The Taylor rule advises the Fed to keep the funds rate high to attract more bank borrowers who produce,[18] but banks prefer a low rate which attracts a larger multitude of borrowers. Too much bank lending then saturates demand, curtails lending, and causes insolvencies which trigger recessions.

As a result, investment has become an unending rollercoaster of business booms and busts. During the last half century, the U.S. experienced a dozen such cycles. Chapter 1 already mentioned the wealth gap the cycles produced: **The richest 10% of society now owns the nation's wealth while the bottom 50% owns little.**

Low-income households earn and spend cash, and inflation shrinks their income until it barely covers the cost of life's necessities. They must hold cash just to deal with the volatility of their existence. What they have saved often dissipates in unforeseen emergencies, as they lack the means to be productive.

> Inflation denies the least fortunate the capital and resources they need to be productive.

For them, borrowing is prohibitively expensive. Inflation is a steady drain on emergency funds, and the loss diminishes the odds of ever escaping from poverty. It is a catch-22 that redistribution of wealth won't rectify. Beating the odds requires extraordinary determination and luck. Without it, people end up on government welfare rolls.

The 2008 Global Financial Crisis was the result of the Fed mismanaging the Taylor guidance, repressing the funds rate, and overleveraging banks. It caused an equity and housing crash that almost ended in a global depression. When banks began defaulting on their nonperforming loans, the Fed started a massive bailout.

The Fed counterfeited trillions of dollars to lend to insolvent banks using a process called *quantitative easing* (QE) using a zero-interest rate policy (ZIRP). This deluge of free money debased the dollar, bloated inflation, and caused a nationwide crisis in commercial real estate.

If the Fed kept the funds rate neutral, and banks lent exclusively to productive enterprises, they would increase the money supply in line with real growth, and inflation would disappear. However, the Fed's low rates stimulate borrowing and discourage growth, which by now has declined to barely 2%.

Banks' credit-based money creation may look innocuous, but it causes severe harm in practice because it: (1) imposes a regressive tax; (2) impoverishes the middle class; (3) causes business cycles; (4) distorts market interest rates; and (5) leads to speculation and unproductive capital churn.

The next chapter examines unproductive capital churn. Money creation exceeds what people can consume, and banks and rich individuals siphon that excess out of the productive economy and use it to trade anything that promises a short-term gain. The stock market is one example of a speculative trading venue.

Chapter 5:
Casino Speculation

Decades of money expansion and the banking cartel's exorbitant windfall profits have transferred more funds into the U.S. financial sector than bankers and their clients can invest rationally. They use that excess to speculate by trading real estate, currencies, equity, and debt contracts— any asset whose price they can inflate by injecting money.

Banks stimulate this game with a flow of credit that raises prices and speculative enthusiasm. They feed the process by underwriting corporate bonds and stocks, and packaging loans, mortgages, and other kinds of private debt into exotic securities tailored to their clients' preferences.

Everybody pretends that the game allocates capital to productive businesses. In truth, the influx of new bank money—rather than the prospect of real returns from production—determines price momentum. As Keynes quipped, *when capital development of a country becomes a byproduct of the activities of a casino, the job is likely to be ill-done.*[19]

And yet, the game serves its purpose by injecting new money into circulation, i.e., increasing the money supply, thereby reducing the interest rate at which people can borrow to repay or roll over their existing loans and remain solvent. The new borrowing boosts income and revenue, and helps other debtors remain solvent as well.

The deluge of money maintains debt in perpetuity. Debtors just borrow to repay previous loans and roll over their debts indefinitely. In this way, debt maintains itself without anybody creating real value or income.

Governments can spend more than tax revenue, but still issue allegedly *riskless* debt because they can roll their debt over and borrow more to service it. Society pays for the deficits with its wealth.

Speculation merely boosts asset prices without generating new capital. The turnover of speculative money and the associated price momentum don't improve asset returns and productivity. In fact, banks' exorbitant profits resulting from their money ownership are a source of inflation and recessions.

Terms like *liquidity trap* and *global savings glut* demonstrate that few people understand the origin and effect of the speculative money that banks and their clients use to bloat the financial sector. The equation of exchange used in GDP accounts ignores speculative money and its effect on money velocity and quantity. The Fed admitted as much in 2006, when it ceased to monitor the money quantity M3.[20]

Alvin Hansen and Lawrence Summers hypothesized that when savings accumulate, but the lending rate is too low to risk capital investment, economies tend to succumb to what they call *secular stagnation*.[21][22]

Hansen promulgated this hypothesis during the Great Depression, when decades of money creation had caused a deluge of speculative money whose collapse dispossessed the middle class. Conditions resembled those of today. The severe capital, wealth, and income inequalities across the population were then and now the fundamental reason for economic stagnation.

Worldwide, speculative money dwarfs the money supply circulating locally. Looking for the best return on investment, speculative money moves in and out of national economies, distorting local conditions. Banks and their favored clients seek out global interest-rate differentials and currency misalignments, trying to profit from what they call the *carry trade.*

Claudio Borio pointed out that speculative money exerts a procyclical, destabilizing influence on business conditions both within nations and globally.[23]

> Extreme bank profits and speculative money destabilize economic and financial activity.

Foreign banks and U.S. bank subsidiaries domiciled overseas create dollars outside of U.S. banking jurisdictions. These dollars first appeared in Europe in the 1950s and were called *Eurodollars.* As Friedman explained, the process uses initial dollar deposits that banks lend to their international clients or affiliates.[24]

One might ignore speculative trading as irrelevant casino entertainment if it didn't further aggravate the business cycles that lending excesses already destabilize. Recessions and asset crashes reinforce each other because they both destroy money and choke off liquidity.

We return to the consequences of instability in Part Four of this book. Part Two focuses on the merits of sound money. In Chapter 6, we examine the closest approximation of this concept—a period during which authorities minimized bank interference and ensured that the money supply remained as constant as circumstances would allow.

As will become evident, stable money has many advantages, including being cost-free and socially optimal, as defined by Friedman.[25] In Murray Rothbard's opinion, money is best managed by the markets, which is what happens when the nominal money supply is fixed.

Part Two:
The Merits of Sound Money

Given the injustices and instability caused by banks' money manipulation, one must ask whether there's a better, socially beneficial way for people to interact with money.

The generally accepted narrative is that money supply must grow in line with commerce to ensure stable purchasing power. In the past, such stability was never more than a promise. The world has lived forever with prices rising and falling, and people have learned to adjust to these price changes when they are slow and relatively predictable.

When the money supply is fixed, price changes naturally adjust purchasing power and real income to align with output. Why not allow markets to determine purchasing power, as Murray Rothbard suggested? Fix the nominal money supply and prevent manipulation. The process would be transparent and so simple that everybody could participate in monitoring it.

To be sure, historical periods during which banks or sovereigns refrained from adding to the money supply have been rare. Fortunately, America's founders were suspicious of banking activity and kept money printing under control, at least for short periods initially. In Chapter 6, we examine such a period to establish a baseline case against which to measure today's situation.

Edward Shaw and Ronald McKinnon coined the technical term *financial repression* to describe the range of policies designed to defraud people of monetary wealth.[2627] Chapter 7 explains how the policy that may seem the most harmless—maintaining stable purchasing power—inflicts a regressive loss as high as 10% on the people who can least afford it.

Money is the central measure of everything we have and do economically, and debasing it distorts and corrupts economic activity. Chapter 8 illustrates two of the most egregious outcomes: Depriving people of their fair wages and of their life savings.

Economic distortions cause permanent structural damage—e.g., wealth inequality, economic inefficiency, and societal strife—that aren't reversed naturally, even when policies change. Chapter 9 summarizes the damage that accumulates during decades of financial repression, which then leads to further policy mistakes in attempts to remedy the damage.

For example, quantitative easing to boost faltering growth invariably ends in misallocation of capital. Chapter 10 identifies business cycle manipulation as a policy that causes asset inflation and disruption of productive activity.

Chapter 6:
The Post-Civil-War Era

The period after the Civil War is known for reconstruction and rehabilitation, not for growth and prosperity. But the end of the war also caused a return to sound money and the gold standard, a shrinkage of the money supply and deflation after the inflation of the war.

Moreover, the war had boosted industrial production. Immigrants and African Americans were seeking employment by the millions. This was the 1865–1879 period which Milton Friedman and Anna Schwartz mention in Chapter 1. Remember they wrote that *it refuted the popular claim that price deflation and rapid economic growth are incompatible.*

Claudio Borio and his colleagues corroborate that view. Their research covers 38 economies over a period of 140 years, and they point out that the claim that deflation impedes economic growth is a fallacy and *derives largely from the Great Depression.*[28] The post-Civil-War era and the periods that the Bank of International Settlements studied benefited from sound money. By contrast, the excessive deflation that caused the Great Depression was the result of excessive money creation and debt.

To be sure, the growth period of the 1870s was far from stable. Railroad speculation and European credit excesses destroyed fortunes in the U.S. There was painful wealth inequality. Mark Twain dubbed this period the *Gilded Age* because he correctly observed the inequality and poverty under the patina of thriving commerce, both in the defeated South and among poor workers in the North.

And yet, the combination of sound money and rapid economic growth created a growth dividend which increased the purchasing power of the middle class—the people who earned, held, and spent the cash—as they benefitted from the productivity they created.

In fact, all incomes increased with the growing purchasing power of wages. Many people founded businesses with start-up capital that they had accumulated. Real economic growth rates in the U.S. were the highest in the country's history, and income per capita surpassed that of Britain.[29]

Participation in this general prosperity wasn't a windfall or welfare gift, but rather the unavoidable consequence of Say's law: Real income grew in line with output. This effect is older than money. Even in a barter economy, a good's value increases with the variety and value of the other goods for which it can be exchanged.

> When the money supply is fixed, productivity growth enriches everyone.

This effect also governs the currency exchange between two nations. If they use sound money, the faster-growing nation's currency appreciates against the slower-growing nation's currency. Money expansion today corrupts this relationship.

In the years between 1865 and 1900, deflation and local capital growth supported those who were able and willing to exploit new opportunities. Savers earned rewards, and nobody wasted their time with efforts to protect cash from inflation.

High wages and opportunities for profit gave everyone a chance to flourish based on their individual abilities. Mild deflation dispersed capital rather than concentrated it among a minority, as inflation does. Wealth inequality and poverty receded rather than grew, as they do today.[30]

Private capital dominated capital markets, and capital returns were high. This outcome undermines today's argument that deflation slows spending and impedes investment. Banks did not create money but intermediated investment. Capital remained in the productive process and didn't benefit only banks' favored clients.

To be sure, other reasons also contributed to the general prosperity in the U.S. during the second half of the 19th century: Railroads, farm machines, and the automobile boosted productivity. Unlike today, everyone could afford the technologies. Today, automation boosts productivity primarily among banks and bank-financed corporations that help themselves to the capital. They use it to replace workers, who then lack the resources to become self-employed.

The period was an illustration of how people can thrive when markets are unadulterated by money creation. Of course, history neither proves nor disproves economic theory, but the following chapters demonstrate that a fixed money supply has merit, not only because it prevents regressive taxation, but also because it minimizes market distortions.

It also conforms to Friedman's concept of socially optimal money. Friedman theorized that money creation must minimize people's cost of holding cash balances.[31] Following this line of argument and recognizing inflation as the cost banks impose on society, we find that society is best served by money that's fixed, owned by the citizenry, and wholly determined by market forces.

Chapter 7 demonstrates that the alternative—keeping the value of money, rather than the quantity of money, stable—leads to confiscation of society's productivity gains because the necessary money expansion transfers the growth-related purchasing power gains from currency holders to banks.

Chapter 7:
The Growth Dividend

The official narrative is that a fixed money supply causes deflation, harms the economy, and diminishes aggregate demand. Banks' true concern is that delinquencies accelerate when deflation decreases borrowers' nominal incomes. Banks expand the money supply to ensure that borrowers service their debts. They don't care that inflation impoverishes low-income consumers.

The correct policy would be to stop expanding the money supply. Economic growth then would increase purchasing power and provide people with a growth dividend, boost consumption, and support employment. The rich would stop chasing unproductive hedges against inflation.

However, banks have convinced the public that deflation is undesirable, and that banks must create money to avoid deflation. People fail to realize that this excuse enriches banks by boosting bank lending rates and bank profits. The growth dividend is a bank windfall that rightfully belongs to society.

Banks can and do increase their windfall profits by adding inflation. The Fed's monetary policy expressly seeks 2% inflation by boosting the money supply in line with economic growth until they extort from the poorest class not only the inflation loss, but also the growth dividend. Both together equal the nominal GDP growth.

In the U.S., money supply growth exceeded $ 1 trillion annually during the 1990s. The cumulative money supply circulating in the U.S. today equals the sum of all past cash holder losses in current dollars—currency, coins, and banknotes. The banking system extorted the wealth that this money represents from the lower middle class.

In practice, poor people suffer a greater loss than that indicated by nominal GDP growth for two reasons: (1) low wage growth, which is discussed in the next chapter, and (2) their need to spend their income predominantly on essentials—shelter, health care, energy, and food—which exhibit substantially higher inflation rates than luxury items.

> Money expansion determines the regressive tax that banks collect.

However, rich people spend their incomes on homes, discretionary goods, and capital assets, whose price increases and returns compensate them for the ongoing debasement of money.

The government reports average price indices and inflation rates. In truth, the price effects experienced by people in the lowest-income group are more than twice the averages. For example, when banks increase the money supply—and nominal GDP—by 5%, they extract at least

10% of what the poor could have spent in the absence of money growth.

The higher a person's income, the greater the opportunity to thwart inflation and use leverage for profit. For each of the past three decades, these gains have doubled the financial industry's size and income. After all, stealing wealth and productivity must make somebody rich. The discrepancy hasn't been lost on those who inexorably have sunk into welfare dependency.

To this day, certain theorists blame sundry, vague flaws in the capitalist system for the wealth inequality that money growth fosters. They claim that some stay poor while others grow rich. That may be so, but sound money would give everybody a fair chance. People rightly suspect that the system is rigged and resent that they're not treated fairly.

In a 2016 speech about economic inequality, then-Federal Reserve Chair Janet Yellen advised *making our economy more rewarding for more of the people.*[32] Well, the Fed is doing the opposite.

Alas, despoiling the poor is only one of banks' disservices to society. As Chapter 8 illustrates, banks also corrupt prices, wages, and interest rates, thereby spreading confusion and mischief throughout the economy.

Chapter 8:
Fair Factor Allocation

Money creation not only results in wealth inequality and poverty, but also corrupts wages and interest rates, and gives banks and owners of capital surreptitious opportunities to profit.

Consider the allocation of costs between labor and capital. When the money supply is fixed, and the economy is growing in real terms, prices decline in line with real economic growth, money's purchasing power increases, and wages and capital returns each experience the same marginal growth rate. Under such conditions, the allocation of costs between labor and capital factors is fair and transparent. It also is difficult to manipulate.

However, money expansion obfuscates factor allocation. During the Great Inflation of the 1970s, labor had enough bargaining power to insist that wages increase in line with prices, but by the 1980s, inflation had eroded millions of middle-class earners' livelihoods, impeded self-employment, and encumbered business startups.

Automation and low foreign wages were destroying U.S. workplaces. U.S. industries slowed the pace of wage increases to better compete with imports. People had to seek corporate employment, subverting labor's bargaining power. A disadvantaged underclass, *the deplorables*, emerged in the U.S. heartland.

Had the world's competing nations not had similarly malleable fiat currencies, banking cartels, and monetary policies, the wage and price discrepancies between them might not have worsened. However, after the U.S. defaulted on the dollar's gold backing in 1971 and suspended the Bretton Woods Agreement in 1973, nations were free to debase their currencies, stifle market forces, and inflate prices.

As a result, full-time workers' real wages in the U.S. failed to increase in line with productivity growth. Wage stagnation contributed to income inequality. The loss harmed the same group of people who already had been dispossessed by banks—the lowest-income cohorts. The tragic spoliation amounted to nearly 15% of income, i.e., more than $1 trillion annually.

That loss put essentials—shelter, energy, health care, and education—out of reach for this increasingly impoverished cohort. Domestic demand in the U.S. suffered. The fact that corporations moved their manufacturing to low-wage countries worsened the predicament.

Even more important was the mismanagement of interest rates on which economic participants rely to borrow and invest.

In a balanced economy, labor supply, technology, and savings are the key factors that determine the economy's intrinsic potential. For example, savings provide capital that complements human effort in production. Knut Wicksell's theory explains how undistorted markets guide and motivate savers to finance the development of capital.[33]

Wicksell compared two real interest rates, one of which savers demand to invest their savings. Called the *money market rate*, it depends on the amount of savings available and on inflation or deflation expected in the future. The second interest rate, the *capital return rate*, is the rate that capital owners expect to earn.

The supply of cash and demand for capital are balanced when the money market rate equals the capital return rate. This equilibrium occurs at the *natural interest rate* (also called r^* or the *neutral interest rate*).

Even in a steadily growing economy, when the capital return rate exceeds that of a stagnant economy, the natural interest rate must be satisfied, i.e., the money market rate must equal the capital return rate. The deflation that growth engenders when the money supply is fixed provides exactly that boost to the real money market rate.

Money expansion subverts the equilibrium by depressing the savings rate. Inflation makes matters even worse. When the natural interest rate is less than the capital return rate, people search for yields by investing in anything, just to protect their money's value.

They bid up the prices of capital assets and anything else that promises a return. They waste capital on projects that are only marginally productive and invest in unproductive wealth to protect themselves against inflation.

Over time, incessant money expansion continues to depress the money market rate ever lower. Capital becomes so cheap that it distorts factor-cost allocation, depresses labor costs, and drives labor replacement. The search for return and yield leads to speculation, an unproductive gamble on asset prices' future performance.

> A growing money glut corrupts prices, wages, interest rates, and capital formation.

Consider the U.S. economy of the past 30 years: The capital return rate has dropped from approximately 6% in the '80s to less than 4% today as the economy has become less efficient. The real money market rate has decreased from 6% to almost zero.

The natural equilibrium rate no longer exists. Banks can hardly stimulate lending, even at these low rates, because they have already flooded the world with so much money that it's being wasted on anything that offers even the slightest yield.

The next chapter sheds more light on how society deals with these distortions and how banks try to expand consumer lending as aggregate demand falters, and the middle class reaches its debt limit. Monetary policy is powerless to reverse the wealth and capital inequality that the Fed has created.

Chapter 9:
The Key to Productivity

Chapter 6 described the 1870s when people were highly productive and blessed with capital, savings, and investment. Real economic growth rates were the highest in U.S. history, and income per capita surpassed that of Britain. The Republic was at peace, and war finance was suspended. We can compare that time to today and ask whether we're better off now and whether reserve banking has rendered us more efficient and productive.

The 1970s made small businesses the primary creators of jobs in the U.S. They spawned corporations that became the envy of the world. However, conditions have changed. Net business formation and related employment growth have turned negative.

National productivity has averaged 2.1% in recent decades, helped by increasing automation. However, small businesses and the self-employed didn't participate in that trend, not because the tools and opportunities for automation weren't available, but because they lacked capital.

To boost their productivity, small companies and the self-employed must generate free cash flow or discretionary income to invest, but excessive inflation has harmed small businesses reducing their discretionary income and curtailing their productivity.

To understand the problem, Hans Theil introduced the statistical concept of *entropy* in 1967 as a measure of wealth uniformity across the populace.[34] The more wealth and capital differs across the populace, the fewer agents have the resources, such as capital and energy to start and run businesses.

To put it differently, *the more access exists to available resources, the greater is the sum of opportunities exploited by a society.*[35] Wealth inequality concentrates resources in fewer hands, thereby reducing productivity. The cause of the wealth gap is the Fed and the banking cartel, overabundant money, inflation, and money debasement.

Compare this situation to capitalist markets based on Say's law and sound money. These markets seek to equalize opportunities and achieve uniformity. Debasing the money supply achieves the opposite effect and worsens the outcome.

In today's world, resources comprise not only technology and capital, but also energy in all its forms. While capital costs have dropped as money has become increasingly abundant, the increasing cost of extracting energy has impaired energy affordability for the lower middle class, further jeopardizing productivity.

Government redistribution of wealth cannot replace capital that businesses need to thrive. The *endowment effect*, the hypothesis that people make more efficient use of things they own, applies to capital as well.[36] Gifts and government handouts are an unreliable capital base for expanding a business.

By the 1980s, the Great Inflation of the 1970s had disappeared, but the structural damage that it had created—wealth inequality and capital waste—remained. By pillaging low-income people, inflation was diminishing consumer demand, and the Fed and the general money glut were depressing money market rates.

By 2005, low rates herded people into consumer debt. The Fed and the government no longer worried about productivity, which had dropped by more than half to 0.8%, with real growth shrinking, causing secular stagnation.

The Fed's concern wasn't oversized bank profits, but the realization that once started, the lending binge had to continue because it boosted the income on which borrowers depended to service and repay their debts. Debt service required incomes to grow as they had in the past.

Thus, the Fed continued to ease credit and urge consumers to borrow and shop to the limits of their credit cards. Wholesale consumer lending replaced the prudent banking of yore. Exporters unloaded their goods on exuberant U.S. consumers—underpriced thanks to low wages abroad.

Low-wage imports caused deflation in the U.S. and reduced the already-understated inflation index further. The Fed could barely reach its 2% inflation target no matter how much it grew the money supply.

By the late '90s, the lower-middle class was beginning to reach its credit limits. Banks started worrying about lending risk and demanded collateral and government guarantees. They urged people to consume the equity in their homes—their only retirement nest egg. The Fed welcomed *mortgage equity withdrawal* as a means of keeping the credit pump going.

To accelerate lending, the Fed removed restrictions on banks, eliminated legal reserve requirements, and ignored banks' increasing leverage. Banks sold questionable loans to unsuspecting investors, off-loading their risk. Lax lending standards eventually crashed the financial system in 2008.

Following the crisis, the Fed gave the credit cycle a last desperate push by doing what Fed member Adolph Miller had deplored as the cause of the 1929 crash: The Fed swapped long-duration Treasury bonds for trillion-dollar counterfeit money at zero interest, which investors used to bid up asset prices to levels reminiscent of the 1929 bubble. The Fed's new name for the practice was *quantitative easing.*

By then, the zero rate had ceased to be an incentive for borrowing. Consumers already had too much debt. Low-income consumers had turned to what Hyman Minsky had called *Ponzi finance*, adding more debt just to service existing liabilities. The dearth of borrowers was slowing U.S. economic growth.

The government stepped in with guarantees, loans, welfare checks, and promises of future assistance. With the economy stagnating, raising taxes would have meant certain recession. Thus, the Fed monetized the public safety net. Friedman used a metaphor for monetized spending, calling it *dropping money from helicopters.*[37]

The government rolled over maturing debt and paid interest by taking on new liabilities. It was another Ponzi scheme. Nobody talked about what most people knew: The nation had no way of repaying its debt.

Worse yet, printing money to pay welfare recipients meant pillaging the shrinking middle class by collecting a regressive inflation tax from those with the lowest incomes. It meant confiscating the discretionary income that people needed to start and grow small businesses--eating the nation's seed corn and adding more people to the welfare rolls.

> Consumer borrowing and deficit spending rob Peter to pay Paul.

The signs of declining trust in money look harmless at first. People see prosperity decline and accelerating inflation in prices of things they need. They then begin to evade taxes, participate in the black market, revert to barter, and invent money substitutes—cryptocurrency being a recent example. As activity shifts to an underground economy, official money is used for fewer transactions, inflation accelerates further, and tax collection declines.

Chapter 10 examines one of the side effects of monetary mismanagement: the business cycle. Often blamed on people's emotions, the business cycle is instead an outgrowth of the absurd money splurge that banks force on society.

Chapter 10:
Business Cycles

In a world of dispossessed and underpaid consumers, credit is a way of raising people's *animal spirits.* [38] For the affluent, it's just a way of life, but for those who live from paycheck to paycheck, the magic of the credit card is a mechanism for enriching banks.

To be sure, the vagaries and delays of price increases and concurrent economic growth obscure the outcome and help sell to consumers the narrative that extravagance is free. However, the fact remains that purchasing power must realign with output, and the growth burst of booming credit must revert to the trend rate of growth.

It makes sense that real economic trend growth is determined entirely by a country's productivity and available labor hours. Accelerating this growth by injecting paper money creates a temporary credit boom followed by the loss of purchasing power and the painful liquidation of excess capacity.

In fact, if people paid attention to the average long-term U.S. economic growth rate, they would see a decelerating trend. Money creation worsens wealth and capital inequality and scuttles entrepreneurial efforts. The result is secular stagnation.

Previous chapters in this book have focused on long-term secular credit trends and intentionally have ignored periodic cycles, which are well-understood, stemming from the haphazard volatility of credit-based money creation. Sound money is a prerequisite for efficient trend growth.

This chapter's purpose is to highlight the harm that business cycles inflict on society.

During a credit boom, people overborrow and overspend in the mistaken hope that the boom will become the new trend. Markets respond by debasing money. Only increased borrowing and money growth can keep the boom going.

Eventually, waning demand ends the boom. Banks anticipate the end and start denying credit. Revenue and income shrink, causing a chain reaction of delinquencies. Irving Fisher called it the *debt-deflation spiral*.[39]

This spiral is the reason why credit busts unravel in panic until the shrinking money supply stabilizes the purchasing power at a lower level. At that point, if the downturn hasn't been too disruptive, healthy businesses recover after excess capital investment is liquidated. Authorities rush to limit the damage, but curtailing it allows misallocated capital and nonperforming loans to linger. Joseph Schumpeter recommended replacing weak firms with new, more productive ones in a process he called *creative destruction*.[40]

New research has demonstrated that the creative aspect of this process depends greatly on the crash, the subsequent recession's duration, and the extent to which it shrinks demand and the money supply.[41] To subdue inflation, the Fed tends to raise the funds rate prior to the crash, which worsens the crash by shutting off bank lending, thereby shrinking the money supply.

Sound money based on a fixed money supply would mitigate, if not prevent, business cycles because excess money is the intrinsically destabilizing factor.

Banks also fan the flames of asset speculation by lending to speculators, trading their own loans to each other, and enticing the public to earn income on speculative investments. When the boom reverses, speculators withdraw their funds, banks stop lending, and insolvencies cause deflation. In this way, banks initiate a downturn more severe than the typical recession.

Abrupt deflation destroys weak, leveraged businesses. The first to suffer are the self-employed and small businesses, which inflation has already weakened during decades of wealth confiscation. Business networks dissolve permanently, and people disperse in search of work elsewhere.

> Business cycles harm those already weakened by prior decades of confiscation.

The leveraged speculation of the 1920s caused a collapse of the money supply so severe that it destroyed the sustenance of the U.S. middle class, which inflation had bled of its savings and wealth during the preceding decades. The 1913 Federal Reserve Act, the U.S. banking cartel, and banks' self-dealing and speculation incited the debt-deflation spiral of the Great Depression.

The 1933 Banking Act, which came to be known as the Glass-Steagall Act, tried to prohibit commercial banks in the U.S. from speculating with their depositors' money. However, Congress repealed this timid prohibition of banks' fraudulent activity in 1999, which promptly led to the financial calamity of 2008.

The Fed's quantitative easing is a way of adding even more speculative tinder while it holds the federal funds rate at zero. The policy causes even more asset inflation, misallocation of capital, accumulation of debt, and wasted wealth and resources.

In Part Four of this book, we return to the theme of banking mischief and what to do about it. Part Three is an excursion into the world of global trade and how fiat money creation has generated irreconcilable tensions in that realm as well.

Part Three:
Money Wars

The End of the dollar's gold backing in 1971 changed the postwar monetary order and convinced the world that the bankers' way of creating money would become a competitive weapon going forward. The world united in abandoning sound money, debasing its currencies, and impoverishing its people.

U.S. bankers had been preparing for this moment since 1913, ready to exploit what foreigners called the nation's exorbitant privilege: creating dollar reserves and dollar assets for the world's competitive activities. Little did U.S. bankers expect—or care—that the activity would disadvantage U.S. citizens.

Domestic easy-money policies had a global corollary: As long as new money kept coming in, everybody remained solvent, and debts could accumulate without short-term repercussions—though they were destined for a distant day of reckoning.

The same addictive lending policies that magnified the differences between rich and poor within nations turned the relationships between nations into irreconcilable credit disputes. Unsurprisingly, some of these relations devolved into competitive money wars.

In Chapter 11, we explore why nations—even those that subscribe to socialist ideologies—impoverish their own citizens for competitive advantage. Currency arrangements among nations are the subject of Chapter 12. We arrive at the conclusion that diverse nations benefit from flexible exchange rates and fixed nominal money supplies: Letting nations adjust to their own natural conditions without money creation would prevent the monetary dystopia that we are experiencing today.

Chapter 11:
Race to the Bottom

The Bretton Woods Agreement, which fixed exchange rates, collapsed in November 1973. From that point onward, each nation could print money as fast as it wanted. For the first time in human history, currency debasement spanned the globe.

The main reason was that postwar demand for reserve dollars had increased dramatically. Global traders found it convenient to price and trade all goods in the same currency. The dollar had been the only gold-backed currency, and everyone knew and trusted it. However, to acquire dollars, foreigners had to sell their goods in the U.S., then pay their local labor in local currency. The resulting inflation confiscated wealth from the domestic population, debased the local currency, and started a process called *competitive devaluation.*

The exporting country converted the acquired dollars into Treasury bonds, thereby lending their profits back to the U.S. government. The global preference for dollars was known as America's *exorbitant privilege:* It supported the value of the U.S. currency and sovereign debt, but depleted U.S. gold reserves.

In 1971, when the U.S. defaulted on gold convertibility, it needed to convince foreigners that U.S. currency and debt would retain their value. The 1974 *petrodollar agreement* served that purpose: Oil exporters promised the U.S. that they would price the world's oil in U.S. dollars and invest them in the U.S. in exchange for U.S. military protection.

At the height of the dollar's popularity, foreign reserve accounts held $8 trillion U.S. bonds—half of U.S. public debt. The exorbitant privilege, speculative bank profits, and the petrodollar—rather than the so-called *global savings glut*— were the reason for low borrowing costs and low inflation in the U.S.

The worldwide need for U.S. dollars was a boon for U.S. banks, and accelerated expansion of the money supply, spread financial repression, and exported inflation. Extravagant spending in the U.S. kept the world trading and U.S. banks raking in profits.

And yet, imperceptibly but irreversibly, the spending increased private debt and ruined U.S. producers, who couldn't compete against low foreign wages and the competitive devaluation of foreign currencies.

David Ricardo's theory of comparative advantage served as the justification for global trade.[42] He argued in 1817 that production occurs where costs are lowest and that trade, therefore, benefits everyone. However, this was before banks created money out of thin air. In 1960, in testimony before the U.S. Congress, Robert Triffin warned that the U.S. would come to regret its exorbitant privilege— and he was right.[43]

The Plaza Accord of 1985 was a belated attempt to deflate the U.S. dollar, i.e., reduce its exchange value to provide some breathing room for U.S. industries. However, the accord was unsuccessful in reversing the habits to which Americans had gotten accustomed over previous decades. Foreign export industries retained their dominance, U.S. consumers maintained their taste for imports, and U.S. banks continued creating U.S. dollars for global trade.

> Money debasement and exorbitant privilege crippled U.S. manufacturing.

Increasingly, U.S. corporations moved manufacturing to low-wage countries, and U.S. labor endured the brunt of the policy that established the U.S. dollar as the reserve currency worldwide. U.S. consumers continued to borrow money, which temporarily subsidized their shrinking incomes, but eventually lined the lenders' pockets.

Over time, exporting countries diversified their reserves and began to accept euros, yen, yuan, and pounds—and recently even gold—in their reserve accounts.

To be sure, nations would have been more careful creating trade imbalances if they had been unable to create money. That would have forced them to lend private savings to foreigners, thereby sacrificing their own capital. Creating money at will allows exporters to lend their citizens' wealth to foreigners without asking when and whether these loans will be repaid.

Today, global trade has declined due to a lack of creditworthy consumers. Central banks try to keep the credit game going by monetizing debt. Nations accelerate competitive devaluation and other mercantilist policies, including tariffs, export subsidies, and outright restrictions on imports. These efforts slowly suffocate trade flows.

A rational approach would be for nations to restrain the money printers, restructure debt, dismantle structural distortions, and refrain from erecting trade barriers. Instead, caught in what game theorists call a *prisoner's dilemma*, each nation protects its own national interests, which shrinks global trade.

If global trade is to avoid periodic crises, monetary relations between nations must change. The next chapter offers some thoughts on this issue.

Chapter 12:
Regional Wealth Gaps

Social mobility used to be an American birthright: People's choices, ambitions, and education determined their wealth and income. Today, regressive confiscation of wealth magnifies differences in income and wealth and restricts mobility. The wealth inequality also shows in the differences between the U.S. coasts and the heartland.

To be sure, the coasts have always been attractive for those looking for opportunities. It's no secret that Wall Street traders earn more than Oklahoma farmhands. New Yorkers habitually invest a large fraction of their income to protect it from inflation.

Inflation harms the people in the heartland. Global competition keeps their wages and job opportunities stagnant. U.S. monetary and industrial policies ignore their plight. Coastal technocrats who used to be their supporters now overlook the *deplorables of flyover America*.

The regressive wealth confiscation caused by inflation and excessive debt destroyed the heartland's economic resilience during the Roaring Twenties, obliterated local commerce in the '30s, and has increased income inequality since the '80s.

Diversity is unavoidable in a country as large as the U.S. despite the benefits of a common language and culture, and the opportunity for people to move and mingle. And yet, banks' money manipulation has magnified wealth inequality in a way that people perceive as underhanded and unfair.

The same dynamic prevails on a global scale. The Bretton Woods Agreement, the gold standard, and Europe's 1992 Maastricht Treaty were supposed to enhance trade by unifying the currency or at least equalizing exchange and interest rates. However, excessive money and debt creation outweighs the benefits of unified trade and capital flows. Debt increases in less productive communities while capital ends up in more productive areas.

This issue haunts especially the eurozone, whose Stability and Growth Pact is unable to align productivity and budgets. Sovereign debts accumulate at different rates while unsatisfactory debt repayment mechanisms create conflicts. [44] The latest eurozone plan is the *European Stability Mechanism,* which seems destined to become a eurozone Department of the Treasury. Whether this mechanism can unify members' productivity and budgets is an open question.

The gold standard ended in a similar predicament when it used exchange rates to enforce sound money supplies. Faster-growing nations had to depreciate their currencies to prevent other members from accumulating debts, forcing prosperous members to grow at the lowest common denominator.

After World War I, when the British Empire ran out of gold to sell, the governor of the Bank of England, bemoaned the problem with the remark: *We collected money from a lot of poor devils and gave it to the four winds.*[45] To put it differently, the gold standard prohibited member nations from growing at their own pace compatible with the wealth and vigor of their land and people.

A monetary system should be designed to provide freedom and diversity to citizens and nations alike. It should mitigate differences, not aggravate them. Fixing the nominal money supply rather than the currency's purchasing power meets these requirements because it allows each national currency to adjust in line with the country's economic growth rate.

A fixed nominal money supply also has merit when diverse regions opt for a common currency. In this case, markets adjust local inflation to regional disparities. For example, New Yorkers would transfer some of their wealth to Oklahomans and thus mitigate geographic differences.

> Flexible exchange rates allow currencies to adjust to nations' natural growth rates.

Tying the currency's purchasing power to gold to prevent national banking cartels from creating money has never worked very well. In today's digital world, it is possible and advisable to prohibit banks—like everybody else—from counterfeiting money.

Gold could serve a valuable purpose as a potential global reserve currency, as it would reveal countries that counterfeit illegally. Keynes suggested such a reserve currency at Bretton Woods, calling it the *bancor.*

Part Four of this book addresses these questions in the context of a new monetary approach that would serve societies rather than banks. To provide background, Chapters 13 and 14 describe details of current banking practices.

Part Four:
The Need for Reform

In the banking business, economies of scale, brand recognition, and client trust reinforce each other. An isolated bank can issue banknotes only to people who trust its capital base. However, people trust a national banking franchise without reservation and rely on its deposit insurance. The organizational structure allows for almost limitless money creation. Luckily, the founders prevented individual banks from uniting prior to 1913.

The cartel that the Federal Reserve Act created in 1913 permanently changed the U.S. economy and ultimately U.S. society, which it split into a capital-starved underclass and a financial elite taking advantage of banks' money creation. Of course, the government is the prime beneficiary, able to increase taxes, its debt and size, and its imperial reach in step with the cartel's credit expansion.

Today, this game is deteriorating even for the key players. There is simply too much debt, wealth inequality, and economic stagnation. Chapters 13, 14, and 15 describe the shortcomings. Past money excess has corrupted not only the economy, but also the banking business. America's founders envisioned an entirely different financial future. Chapter 16 recommends desirable corrective actions.

Chapter 13:
Fiduciary Neglect

Money is a common good whose stability affects people's well-being and prosperity. If its custody is left to private interests, the money supply becomes unstable. America's founders understood this fact and charged Congress with stewardship of money.

During the first century of the Republic, banks issued *fiduciary notes* that provided liquidity for trusted clients. Only banks that backed these notes with capital could circulate them in lieu of fiat money. Strict laws and court supervision protected this fiduciary relationship.

The capital held in abeyance by these banks ensured that the addition of notes in circulation did not add to the money supply. In 1836, the U.S. government refused to recharter the Second Bank of the United States, which had cooperated with other banks to violate these rules.

After the 1913 banking reform, the government declared all bank notes legal tender which convinced people and even the judiciary that the Fed supervised fiduciary vigilance, not by the courts.

The Federal Reserve proceeded to counterfeit paper dollars for banks to loan. Banks gambled with their own and their clients' money, eventually leading to the Great Crash of 1929. The government responded by guaranteeing part of people's bank deposits—a measure that prompted banks to take even greater risks.

The U.S. default on gold convertibility removed the last restriction on fiat money. The Fed's counterfeiting backed base money and reserves, and the funds rate determined credit creation. The Fed allowed lending to accelerate until households began to reach their credit limits and slowed the turnover of money.

When the Keynesian Fed tried to boost demand further by lowering rates, speculative money proliferated, credit risks skyrocketed, lending became less profitable, and banks added other activities to their business model.

Today, commercial banks are engaged not only in fractional-reserve banking, but their capital also must cover the risks of trading, insurance, and foreign exchange, just to name a few activities. They compute their total *value at risk* by assigning risk weights to individual assets and to the offsetting hedges.

The proliferation of speculative dollars isn't limited to the U.S. The ubiquitous global trade in dollars has prompted banks in other countries to manage dollars as well. Exporting and importing firms in these countries and their foreign clients take advantage of loosely organized bank alliances that create Eurodollars.

Just like any other fractional-reserve system, bank alliances rely on U.S. dollars as reserves to facilitate interbank movements of Eurodollars. The reserves serve as limits to Eurodollar creation, making the Eurodollar supply sensitive to dollar flows out of the U.S.

When the 2008 Global Financial Crisis shrank the flow of dollars from the U.S. banking system, Eurodollar creation suffered, as did global trade. The crisis was a compelling example of the destabilizing effect that fractional-reserve banking can exert on the money supply, trade, and economic stability.

The next chapter focuses on the Fed's influence, its own money creation, and how its misguided policies caused egregious policy failures of what should have been its most important mandate: managing money in a way that benefits society and increases productivity.

Chapter 14:
Financial Anarchy

Banks are private, for-profit corporations that lend money when they have creditworthy clients and enough capital to remain solvent. Banks own the Federal Reserve, which supports their business. The government benefits from banks' money creation, is their most active borrower and the most prolific spender of their loans.

But the government promises not to interfere in the Fed's money creation. Of course, that promise has its limits: When the government wanted to default on its war bonds, it had the Fed launch the Great Inflation of the 1970s.

When the government wanted to stimulate growth, it had the Fed depress interest rates, which choked off banks' profits.[46] In response, U.S. bankers lobbied for the Gramm-Leach-Bliley Act which allowed banks in 1999 to enter any business from asset and derivatives trading to insurance and underwriting.

> Too much money creation increased lending risk and bank speculation.

With these new options available to them, U.S. banks' interest in money lending declined. Money creation via collateralized *repurchase agreements*, i.e., *repos,* allowed banks to create *shadow money* outside of their balance sheets. By using the same collateral multiple times—a process called *rehypothecation*—banks boosted their profits.

During the heyday of Eurodollar lending, Eurodollar banks used dollars that originated in the U.S. and multiplied them 1.5 times. That meant they created *offshore dollars* by multiplying their U.S. reserves 3×2×1.5 times: When the Fed created one U.S. reserve dollar, the banks launched nine U.S. dollars into circulation.

However, money creation was only a small part of U.S. banks' business. Computers provided inside information that enabled banks to anticipate and bet on the momentum created by speculative markets. Banks profited from lending to their clients, from commissions on their clients' trading activities, and directly from their own bets. Unsuspecting retail investors were the losers.

The trading activity leveraged asset speculation and inflated asset prices, making asset bubbles more severe. Contractions shocked the productive economy and caused lasting damage. Crashes particularly tended to harm those stripped of capital and savings by wealth confiscation and wealth inequality.

Banks, the appointed guardians of stable money, became the worst violators of money stability. By flooding U.S. banks with reserves, the Fed perpetuated cyclicality and volatility, bailed out banks without penalty, and encouraged banks to take excessive risks, which exacerbated credit booms and busts.

And yet, the Fed keeps blaming WWI for the Great Depression of the 1930s, WWII for the Great Inflation of the 1970s, and bank leverage for the Great Recession of 2008. It refuses to accept that its own policies have subjected U.S. society to the worst wealth inequality.

Chapter 15 summarizes the untenable conditions that unbridled money creation has now forced on the world twice in barely a century.

Chapter 15:
Warning Signs

Today, conditions in the U.S. seem surprisingly like those of the Roaring Twenties. Money creation has stripped the lower middle class of its productive resources, and a bank-supported upper crust spends its spoils on flipping stocks, mansions, and fine art, while the money glut is of little help to the rest of the shrinking middle class.

Speculative money finances malls, hospitals, and university campuses, hoping that the government will keep supporting pensions, health care, and student loans so that the buildings earn the rent needed to repay their cost.

Today's conditions may be even more precarious than they were in the 1920s. People live longer, and the birth rate is declining. Foreign currency manipulation is destroying domestic industries. The bureaucracy's regulatory overreach is choking off the formation and growth of productive businesses.

To prevent their debt-heavy economies from stalling, central banks in the U.S., Japan, the eurozone, and China are practicing quantitative easing in hopes of rekindling a worldwide credit boom. However, with consumers tapped out, the money glut expands asset bubbles.

Central banks fail to recognize that they cannot reverse the structural inequality and resultant economic stagnation that they have created. U.S. public debt is now 120% of GDP, and the income from incremental growth of U.S. output cannot service this debt. The Fed monetizes fiscal overspending and tries to shrink government deficits by debasing the currency.[47] Alas, inflation postponed is not inflation eschewed.

To be sure, a rich country can suffer decades of monetary mismanagement before wealth and resources are so thoroughly destroyed that people give up on their money. However, the process accelerates when money manipulation, wealth inequality, and periodic booms and busts relegate a growing segment of society to welfare benefits.

Severe financial events can push latent weakness into permanent collapse. Japan suffered such an event in 1991, the U.S. in 2008, and the eurozone in 2013. Fortunately, the West avoided a disruption such as the Great Crash of 1929 with the help of modern countercyclical stabilizers, fiscal safety nets, deposit insurance, and bank bailouts.

However, there is no doubt that asset bubbles and credit booms reinforce each other and steepen and accelerate normal business downturns to such an extent that commerce fails to adjust. Entire supply chains stop functioning, and unemployment diminishes consumption and further shrinks the money supply. Income and output decline rapidly.

People harmed by wealth confiscation lack the cash reserves to sustain commerce during normal downturns.

The volatility of the credit-based money creation process transforms a natural economic downturn into long-lasting stagnation and sometimes permanent retrogression.

The Bank for International Settlements wrote in its 2015-2016 annual report that *misallocations that occur during a boom [and] the corresponding effects on productivity growth can be substantial, [weakening] the recovery.*[48]

The evidence is unmistakable. The crashes of 1929 in the U.S. and 1991 in Japan destroyed middle-class productivity. A similar, though less abrupt, productivity decline in the U.S. occurred after the 2008 Global Financial Crisis. The decades that followed all saw the same economic stagnation.

> Declines in middle-class productivity followed the 1929 and 2008 downturns.

The Great Depression ended in 1941 with the government taking control of industry, finance, and capital as the U.S. entered WWII. Wealth inequality disappeared, and the postwar effort rehabilitated the middle class. However, the waste of resources was so enormous that it took until 1975 for inflation to cancel the war debt.

Today, Federal Reserve policy has left the U.S. in even worse shape and burdened it with more debt than in the '70s. Thoughts on how to reverse these misguided policies, reform the financial sector, and correct the egregious distortions of the past century are the subject of Chapter 16.

Chapter 16:
Debt and Delusion

The income tax, which President Wilson introduced in 1913 was minute, about 1% of earnings. Since then, credit expansion has enabled the government to double its size and revenue nearly every decade. Today, 3 million civil servants spend annual tax receipts of $4.4 trillion. In addition, they borrow trillion-dollar deficits every year to expand regulation and supervision of the private sector.

> The federal government owes $34 trillion Treasury debt and $100 trillion of other liabilities, such as Social Security, Medicare, and Medicaid.

The government spends what it borrows and produces little, which results in inflation and debases the currency, people's incomes, and debts. [49] The reason for the anemic growth is the Fed's low rate which incites borrowing and discourages saving, investment, and production.

Additional impediments are the aging society, the skills gap, the declining workforce, an abundance of retirees, and the lowest birth rate in a century. They offer little hope that growth will rebound and require a high interest payment on the debt **which amounts to $1 trillion.**

The federal treasury must roll over a large fraction of the federal debt every year. A lack of creditors forces the

Fed to monetize part of the debt, a process which devalues the currency, poses a trenchant crisis for the fiat dollar, and keeps creditors wary.

Foreigners used to have great esteem for the U.S. financial infrastructure and its banking and legal systems. They used to have respect for U.S. privileges and prerogatives. However lately, the U.S. weaponized its financial activities by imposing trade sanctions to enforce its authority.

For example, the U.S. government confiscated Russian sovereign reserves in U.S. banks, among them U.S. Treasurys. With this action, the U.S. effectively defaulted on debt it owes Russia, another sovereign nation. Unsurprisingly, foreign U.S. creditors took immediate notice of this infringement on international law.

The *BRICS+ and OPEC+* nations, which own most of the world's energy and gold resources, are revising their petrodollar policy.[50] Central banks worldwide are replacing reserve dollars with gold bullion. Foreign dollar holdings are still plentiful, but America's creditors have second thoughts.

How geopolitical changes evolve and affect U.S. financial conditions is as yet unclear, but the U.S. financial and banking systems will certainly face challenges.

Here is a list of recommendations which would correct some shortcomings of the U.S. financial system:

o Stricter control of counterfeiting and money expansion is necessary to keep the fiat money system in operation.
o Low funds rates and quantitative easing are counterproductive because they cause more debt and less production.
o Savings and capital growth must be strengthened by keeping rates high and close to Wicksell's natural rate.
o Congress must embrace its constitutional responsibility and oversight of U.S. money.
o Governance of U.S. finances, taxing, borrowing, and budgeting, needs better coordination.
o Public instead of bank ownership of money would reduce the heavy cost banks impose on productivity.
o The enormous wealth that banks have siphoned from the productive sector should be returned to society to help restructure and retire public and private debt.
o As Robert Triffin correctly predicted, the dollar's reserve status harmed the U.S. economy. A new reserve currency based on special drawing rights (SDRs), backed by gold, would enhance stability and guard against excessive counterfeiting.

If the fiat dollar is to survive, the U.S. must find a way back to the founders' intent and rationale. Sound money, a free-market economy, a neutral money rate, and clear responsibilities will be essential. Citizens must relearn to save and invest in productive capital to spawn a productive revival.

The following postscript lists some reasons why the 1913 reforms evolved the way they did and how America should be able to avoid the fate of other fiat currencies.

Postscript:
Fighting the Fiat Fate

Europe's banks have manipulated European money supplies for centuries—interrupted only by the gold standard which, for a time, enforced sound money. When bankers are in charge, they blame capitalism for instability and claim they stabilize capitalism and inequality and poverty are simply the price that society must pay for the bankers' patronage.

Don't believe it.

The reverse view—that banks' money creation destabilizes capitalism—is closer to the truth. This argument is based on the premise that the value of money derives from the exchange of goods. [51] Hence, adding to the money supply changes the value of the money units and confounds money interactions. As Jean Baptiste Say explained, only sound money accomplishes a fair distribution of the fruits of productivity.

Surreptitious manipulation of money is as old as money itself. Nations used it to fund armies, annex colonies and found empires while impoverishing their citizens. Fractional reserve banking only increased the unabashed use and extent of money manipulation. America must learn to control this abuse.

When Mahatma Gandhi visited London in1947, he was aghast at the poverty of the empire's citizens. British academics blamed capitalism for their fellow citizens' misery and kept quiet about the British banking cartel's massive counterfeiting, inflation, and money debasement that paid for their wars.

No wonder that Europe's huddled masses responded to the call of a nation whose constitution clearly rejected the European banking machinations. The U.S. punished counterfeiting as severely as treason and promised to keep people's money safe. America must return to this promise.

George Wahington chose a treasury secretary who promised to safeguard the new nation's money supply. When he reluctantly authorized the First Bank of the United States, Congress repealed its charter when it began abusing its printing powers.

Because printing money proved so much easier than taxation, Congress chartered a Second Bank of the United States in 1816, which had 25 branch offices and the power to regulate private banks. The bank's money printing led to the Western land rush, the Panic of 1819, and the bank's closure in 1832.

Civil War financing was the precedent that helped U.S. bankers succeed in their third attempt to impose a European banking system on the U.S. with all the trappings that haunt people to this day.

President Woodrow Wilson, a former law professor at Princeton University, was more interested in European academics' socioeconomic agenda than in monetary details. He felt that a government-sanctioned banking structure would benefit his WWI preparations. His government endorsement was exactly what bankers desired.[52]

However, President Wilson's actions were harmful. He ignored the Constitution, shifted monetary responsibility to banks, and turned Congress into the irresponsible spender it is today. Europeans were accustomed to banking cartels usurping sovereign prerogatives, and Wilson condoned the system's legal ambiguity in the U.S. Hence, U.S. citizens believe today that counterfeiting is a banking prerogative.

When banks manipulate the money supply, they distort market forces—interest rates, prices, wages, and capital costs. The system then distributes wealth unevenly; inequities accumulate and lead to disaffection among the populace.

The administrative state takes advantage of this chaos by colluding with the banking system which monetizes its deficits and impoverishes its citizens. George Washington said in his Presidential Farewell Address: *Europe has a set of primary interests, which to us have none or very remote relations.* Americans should be proud of American liberty and self-reliance and suspicious of European banking practices.

Bibliography

Brown, Brendan. *A Global Monetary Plague: Asset Price Inflation and Federal Reserve Quantitative Easing*. London: Palgrave Macmillan, 2015.

Cantillon, Richard. *An Essay on Economic Theory*. Auburn, AL: Mises Institute, 2010.

Fisher, Irving. "The Debt–Deflation Theory of Great Depressions." *Econometric Society* 1, no. 4 (1933): 337–357.

Friedman, Milton. *The Optimum Quantity of Money and Other Essays*. Chicago: Aldine, 1969.

Friedman, Milton. "The Euro-Dollar Market: Some First Principles." *Morgan Guaranty Survey*, Morgan Guaranty Trust Company, October 1969. http://research.stlouisfed.org/publications/review/71/07/Principles_Jul1971.pdf, accessed July 31, 2017.

Friedman, Milton, and Anna J. Schwartz. *A Monetary History of the United States, 1867–1960*. Princeton: Princeton University Press, 1963.

Galbraith, John Kenneth. *Money: Whence It Came and Where It Went*. Boston: Houghton Mifflin, 1975.

Hansen, Alvin H. "Economic Progress and Declining Population Growth." *American Economics Review* 29, no. 1 (1939): 1–15. http://www.jstor.org/stable/1806983, accessed July 31, 2017.

Kahneman, Daniel, Jack Knetsch, and Richard Thaler. "Experimental Tests of the Endowment Effect and the Coase Theorem." *Journal of Political Economy* 98, no. 6 (1990): 1325–1348.

Keynes, John M. *The Economic Consequences of Peace*. New York: Harcourt, Brace, and Howe, 1920.

Keynes, John M. *The General Theory of Employment, Interest, and Money*. London: Palgrave Macmillan, 1936.

Lindert, Peter H., and Jeffrey G. Williamson. *Unequal Gains: American Growth and Inequality Since 1700*. Princeton: Princeton University Press, 2016.

Maddison, Angus. *Contours of the World Economy, 1–2030 AD*. Oxford: Oxford University Press, 2007.

McLeay, Michael, Amar Radia, and Ryland Thomas. "Money Creation in the Modern Economy." *Quarterly Bulletin*. Bank of England, 2014 Q1. http://www.bankofengland.co.uk/publications/Pages/quarterlybulletin/2014/qb14q1.aspx, accessed July 31, 2017.

Ricardo, David. *The Works of David Ricardo, Esq., M.P. With a Notice of the Life and Writings of the Author*. Edited by J. R. McCulloch. London: John Murray, 1846.

Rothbard, Murray N. *What Has the Government Done to Our Money?* Auburn, AL: Mises Institute, 1963.

Rothbard, Murray N. "The Origins of the Federal Reserve." *Quarterly Journal of Austrian Economics* 2, no. 3 (1999): 3–51.

Schumpeter, Joseph A. *Capitalism, Socialism, and Democracy*. London: Routledge, 1942.

Snodgrass, Mary Ellen. *Coin and Currency: An Historical Encyclopedia*. Jefferson, NC, and London: McFarland, 2007.

Summers, Lawrence. "The Age of Secular Stagnation: What It Is and What to Do About It." *Foreign Affairs*, March/April 2016.

Wicksell, Knut. *Interest and Prices*. New York: Sentry, 1936.

Yellen, Janet. "Perspectives on Inequality and Opportunity from the Survey of Consumer Finances," Speech to the Conference on Economic Opportunity and Inequality, Federal Reserve Bank of Boston; Boston, MA; October 17, 2014. https://www.federalreserve.gov/newsevents/speech/yellen20141017a.htm, accessed August 7, 2017.

Notes

[1] Thomas Jefferson's letter to John Taylor, 1816.

[2] Thomas Jefferson's letter to Albert Gallatin, 1803

[3] John K. Galbraith. *Money. Whence It Came and Where It Went* (Boston: Houghton Mifflin, 1975), 5.

[4] Ryan Grim. Priceless: "How the Federal Reserve Bought the Economics Profession." (*Huffington Post*, 10-23-2009).

[5] Jean-Baptiste Say. Traité d' Économie Politique, 1803.

[6] Murray N. Rothbard. *What Has Government Done to Our Money?* Auburn, AL: Mises Institute, 1963.

[7] Milton Friedman and Anna J. Schwartz. *A Monetary History of the United States. 1867-1960.* (Princeton University Press, 1963), 29.

[8] Richard Cantillon. Essai sur la Nature du Commerce en Général. (1755) (*An Essay on Economic Theory).* Auburn, AL: Mises Institute, 2010.

[9] Marijn A. Bothuis, Judd N. L. Cramer, Karl O. Schulz, Lawrence H. Summers. "The Cost of Money Is Part of the Cost of Living: New Evidence on the Consumer Sentiment Anomaly." (National Bureau of Economic Research, February 2024). Working Paper 32163.

[10] Carmen Reinhart and Kenneth Rogoff. *This Time Is Different: Eight Centuries of Financial Folly.* (Princeton University Press, 8-7-2011).

[11] G. Edward Griffin. *The Creature From Jekyll Island: A Second Look at the Federal Reserve* (American Media, 1994.)

[12] Garet Garrett. *The Bubble That Broke the World, 1932.* (Mises Institute).

13 Alan Greenspan. "Gold and Economic Freedom." *The Objectivist* 5, no. 7 (1966): 11-15.

14 A. Miller. U.S. Senate, Operations of the National and Federal Reserve Banking Systems, Hearing before a Subcommittee of the Committee of Banking and Currency. (Washington D.C.: U.S. Printing Office, 1931), 134.

15 Meyer Amschel Rothschild. Quote.

16 Jeremy Grantham. Interview, PBS "Frontline" documentary, 2023.

17 Thomas E. Woods Jr. Meltdown: A Free-Market Look at Why the Stock Market Collapsed, the Economy Tanked, and the Government Bailouts Will Male Things Worse. Amazon Kindle Edition. https://www.amazon.com/meltdown.

18 John B. Taylor. "Discretion Versus Policy Rules in Practice." Carnegie-Rochester Conference Series on Public Policy 39, 1993), 193-214.

19 John M. Keynes. *The General Theory of Employment, Interest, and Money* (London: Palgrave Macmillan, 1936), 159.

20 U.S. Federal Reserve. "H.6 Money Stock Measures: Discontinuance of M3,"November 10, 2005 (Revised March 9, 2006).

21 Alvin H. Hansen. "Economic Progress and Declining Population Growth," *American Economics Review* 29, no. 1 (1938): 1-15.

22 Laurence Summers. "The Age of Secular Stagnation: What It Is and What to Do About It." *Foreign Affairs,* March/April 2016.

23 Claudio Borio. "The International Monetary and Financial System: Its Achilles Heel and What to Do About It," BIS Working Paper 456, Bank of International Settlements, August 2014.

24 Milton Friedman. "The Euro-Dollar Market: Some First Principles," Morgan Guarantee Survey, Morgan Guarantee Trust Company, October 1969.

25 Milton Friedman. *The Optimum Quantity of Money and Other Essays* (Chicago: Aldine, 1969).

[26] Edward Shaw. *Financial Deepening in Economic Development* (Oxford: Oxford University Press, 1973).

[27] Ronald McKinnon. "Money and Capital in Economic Development." (Washington: Brookings Institute, 1973).

[28] Claudio Borio, Magdalena Erdem, Andrew Filardo, and Boris Hoffmann. "The Costs of Deflations: A Historical Perspective," *BIS Quarterly Review*, Bank of International Settlements, March 31, 2015

[29] Angus Maddison. *Contours of the World Economy, 1-2030AD* (Oxford: Oxford University Press, 2007), 69.

[30] Peter H. Lindert and Jeffrey G. Williamson. *Unequal Gains: American Growth and Inequality Since 1700* (Princeton: Princeton University Press, 2016).

[31] Friedman, *The Optimum Quantity of Money And Other Essays.*

[32] Janet Yellen, "Perspectives on Inequality and Opportunity From the Survey of Consumer Finances," Speech to the Conference on Economic Opportunity and Inequality, Federal Reserve Bank of Boston, Boston MA, October 17, 2014, https://www.federalreserve.gov/newsevents/speech/yellen20141017a.htm

[33] Knut Wicksell. Interest and Prices, (New York: Sentry, 1936), 102.

[34] Hans Thiel. *Economics and Information Theory* (Amsterdam: North-Holland, 1967).

[35] Detlef Gloge. *Money Forensics: The Looting of Your Birthright.* (Bradenton: Booklocker.com, 2014).

[36] Daniel Kahneman, Jack Knetsch, and Richard Thaler. "Experimental Tests of the Endowment Effect and the Coase Theorem." *Journal of Political Economy* 98, no. 6 (1990): 1325-1348.

[37] Friedman, *Optimum Quantity of Money.*

[38] Keynes, *The General Theory of Employment. Interest, and Money*, 161-162.

[39] Irving Fisher. "The Debt-Deflation Theory of Great Depressions," *Econometrica* 1, no. 4 (1933): 337-357.

[40] Joseph A. Schumpeter. *Capitalism, Socialism, and Democracy*. (London: Routledge, 1942), 83-4.

[41] Ricardo J. Caballero and Mohamad L. Hammour. "The Cost of Recessions Revisited: A Reverse Liquidationist View." *Review of Economic Studies* 72, no. 2 (2005): 313-41.

[42] Ricardo, Works of David Ricardo, 220.

[43] International Monetary Fund, "System in Crisis (1959-1971)," Money Matters: An IMF Exhibit—The Importance of Global Cooperation.

[44] Hans-Werner Sinn, The Euro Trap: On Bursting Bubbles, Budgets, and Beliefs (Oxford: Oxford University Press, 2014).

[45] "Lords of Finance," *The Economist,* January 10, 2009.

[46] Alan Greenspan, "The Challenge of Central Banking in a Democratic Society," Annual Dinner and Fracis Boyer Lecture of the American Enterprise Institute for Public Policy Research, Washington, D.C., December 5, 1996.

[47] Thomas Sargent and Neil Wallace, "Some Unpleasant Monetarist Arithmetic," Federal Reserve Bank of Minneapolis Quarterly Review 5, no. 3 (1981): 2.

[48] Bank of International Settlements, 86th Annual Report, 2015/2016, June 26, 2016, 12.

[49] Carmen M. Reinhart and Belen Sbrancia, "The Liquidation of Government Debt," NBER Working Paper 16893 March 2011.

[50] S. Glazyev and D. Mityaev. Golden Rouble 3.0: How Rusia can Change Foreign Trade Infrastructure. (vedomosti 2022). Vedomosti.ru/opinion/columns/2022/12/27/957178 – zolotoi – ruble).

[51] Percy L. Greaves, Jr., "The Theory of Money," Mises Daily Articles, August 31, 2012, https://mises.org/library/theory-money, accessed August 7, 2017.

[52] Murray N. Rothbard, "The Origins of the Federal Reserve," *Quarterly Journal of Austrian Economics* 2, no. 3 (1999): 3-51.

www.ingramcontent.com/pod-product-compliance
Lightning Source LLC
Chambersburg PA
CBHW071214220526
45468CB00002B/597